Universal Edition

CW00708412

FLORIAN BRAMBÖCK
CELTIC
FLUTE
Duets

www.**universal**edition.com

vienna · london · new york

UE 33 040

ISMN M-008-07788-3
UPC 8-03452-06150-2
ISBN 978-3-7024-3148-8

Vorwort

Celtic Music – das ist die faszinierende Mystik, sind die eingehenden Melodien und teils eigenwillig betonten Rhythmen der traditionellen Musik Irlands, Schottlands und der Bretagne. Ursprünge dieser Musik sind rhythmische Gesangsstücke, welche zunächst nicht instrumental begleitet wurden. Erst im 18. Jahrhundert kamen die bis heute typischen Instrumente wie z.B. Fiddle (Geige), Tin Whistle (Metallflöte), Bodhran (Irische Rahmentrommel) und Uilleann Pipes (Dudelsack) zum Einsatz und gaben dieser Volksmusik ihren charakteristischen Klang. Beliebte Melodiearten bzw. Rhythmen der Celtic Music sind Reel, Jig, Hornpipe und Polka.

Im Gefühl liegt das eigentliche Geheimnis der Celtic Music – sie kommt aus dem Bauch. Melodien und Texte sind untrennbar miteinander verbunden und berühren die Seele des Hörers. Die Liedtexte zu den in diesem Heft verwendeten Stücken findest du ganz leicht im Internet. Viel Spaß beim Singen und Spielen!

Florian Bramböck, April 2006

Preface

Celtic Music, in all its diversity – its mysticism, catchy tunes and, at times, its characteristically accentuated rhythms, is the traditional music from many parts of the British Isles and Brittany. The roots of this music are found in rhythmical songs, originally without instrumental accompaniment. The instruments we consider typical today were only added during the 18th century, namely, the fiddle, tin whistle, bodhran (an Irish frame drum) and the uilleann pipes (a bagpipe). They lend this folk music its characteristic sound. Popular kinds of melodies or rhythms of Celtic Music are the reel, jig, hornpipe and polka.

The true secret of Celtic Music lies in the emotion – it's an instinctive kind of music. Melodies and lyrics are inseparably linked and reach out to the soul of every listener. You will easily find the lyrics to the pieces used in this volume on the internet. Enjoy singing and playing them!

Florian Bramböck, April 2006

PREFACE

La musique celte – synonyme de mystique fascinante, mélodies émouvantes, rythmes parfois singulièrement accentués de la musique traditionnelle d'Irlande, d'Ecosse et de Bretagne. Les origines de cette musique remontent aux chants rythmiques, à l'origine sans accompagnement instrumental. Ce n'est qu'au 18ème siècle que les instruments restés typiques jusqu'à nos jours tel que le fiddle (violon), le tin whistle (flûte métallique), le bodhran (tambour sur cadre) et l'uilleann pipes (cornemuse) sont entrés en scène pour conférer à cette musique populaire le son si caractéristique. Les genres de mélodies et rythmes si populaires de la musique celte sont le reel, le jig, le hornpipe et la polka.

Le vrai secret de la musique celte est dans le sentiment – elle provient du plus profond de nous-mêmes. Les mélodies et les textes sont inséparables et touchent l'âme de l'auditeur. Vous trouverez facilement sur Internet les textes des morceaux publiés dans le présent cahier. Je vous souhaite beaucoup de plaisir à chanter et à jouer!

Florian Bramböck, Avril 2006

Inhalt · Contents · Table des matieres

The Golden Jubilee • 1

The Foggy Dew • 2

My Bonnie Lies Over the Ocean • 4

John Riley • 6

The Wild Rover • 8

Tax Free Should Be All the Music • 10

Danny Boy • 12

Molly Malone • 14

The Old Triangle • 16

The Great Silkie • 18

Drink Your Mighty Lemonade • 20

The Minstrel Boy • 22

Auld Lang Syne • 23

Slievenamon • 26

My Luv is Like a Red, Red Rose • 28

Dance on the Shannon • 30

Loch Lomond • 32

THE GOLDEN JUBILEE

Traditional
arr. Florian Bramböck

Universal Edition UE 33 040

THE FOGGY DEW

Traditional
arr. Florian Bramböck

My Bonnie Lies Over The Ocean

Traditional
arr. Florian Bramböck

John Riley

Traditional
arr. Florian Bramböck

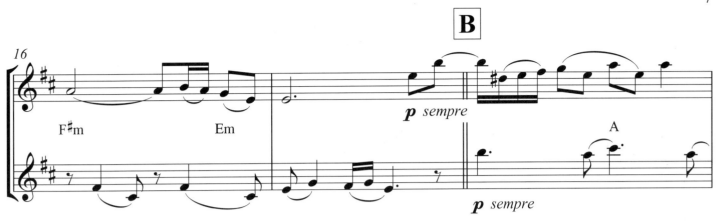

THE WILD ROVER

Traditional
arr. Florian Bramböck

Joyfully waltzing in an Irish Pub ♩=155

TAX FREE SHOULD BE ALL THE MUSIC

Music: Florian Bramböck

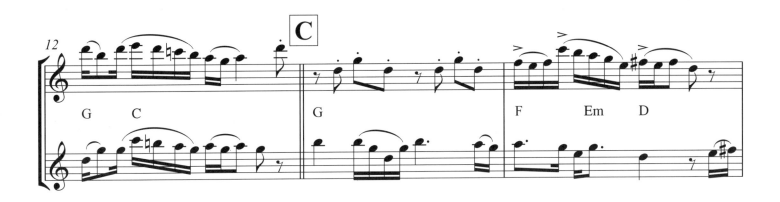

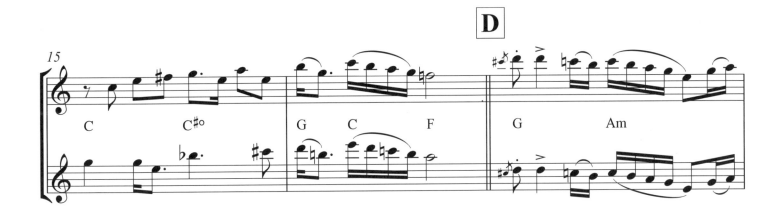

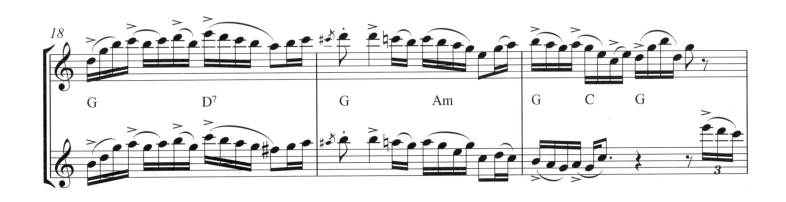

Danny Boy

Traditional
arr. Florian Bramböck

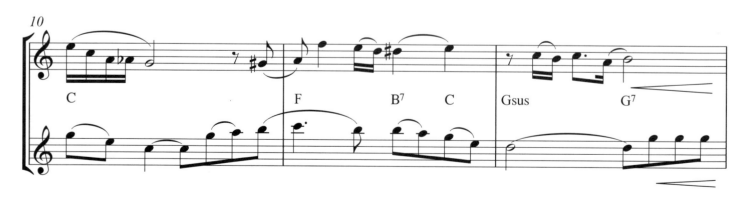

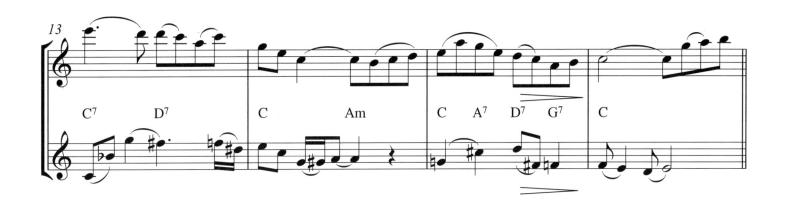

B

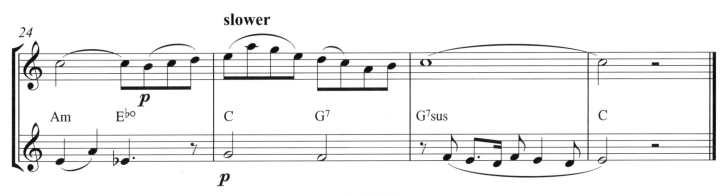

MOLLY MALONE

Traditional
arr. Florian Bramböck

Lively waltz ♩=160 (♩.=54)

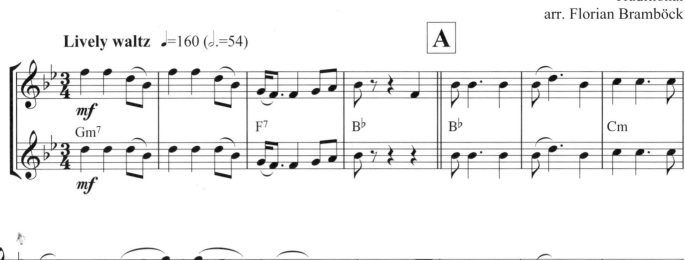

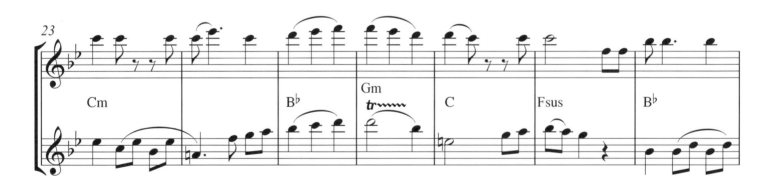

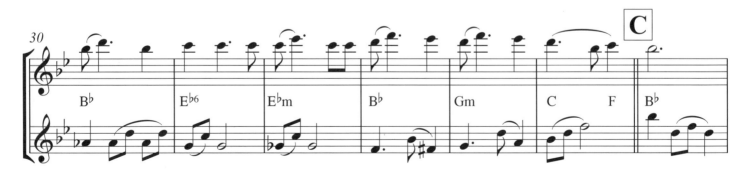

15

THE OLD TRIANGLE

Traditional
arr. Florian Bramböck

The Great Silkie

Traditional
arr. Florian Bramböck

Drink Your Mighty Lemonade

(dance on the gweebarra)

Music: Florian Bramböck

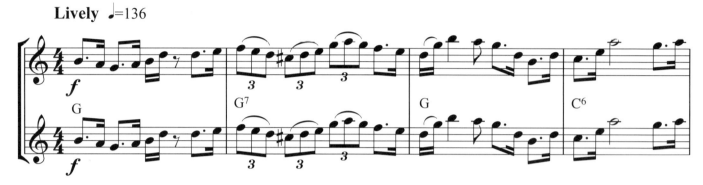

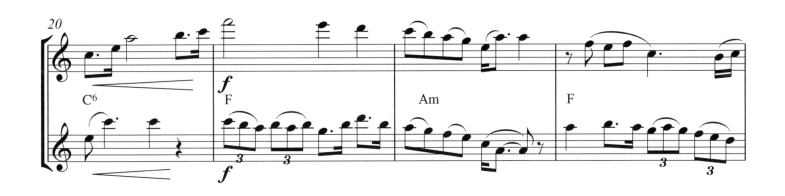

THE MINSTREL BOY

Traditional
arr. Florian Bramböck

Auld Lang Syne

Traditional
arr. Florian Bramböck

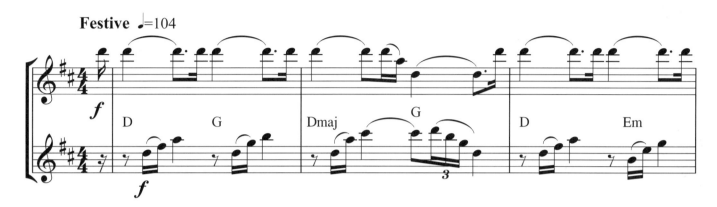

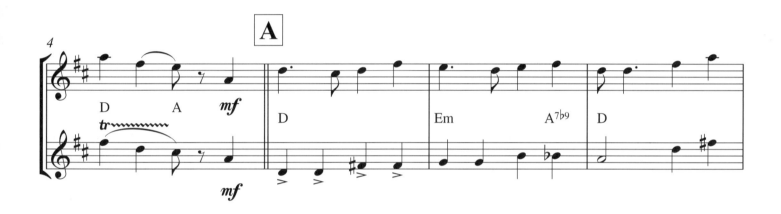

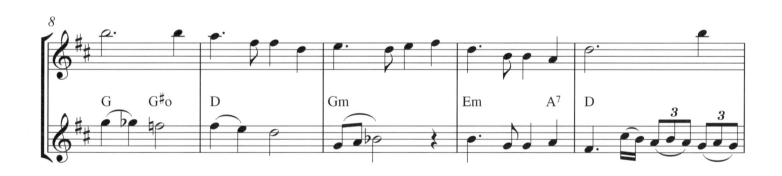

UE 33 040

Slievenamon

Traditional
arr. Florian Bramböck

My Luv Is Like A Red, Red Rose

Traditional
arr. Florian Bramböck

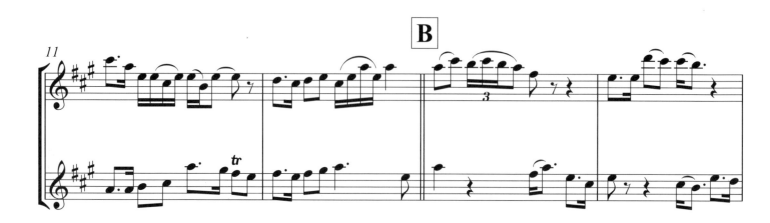

DANCE ON THE SHANNON

Music: Florian Bramböck

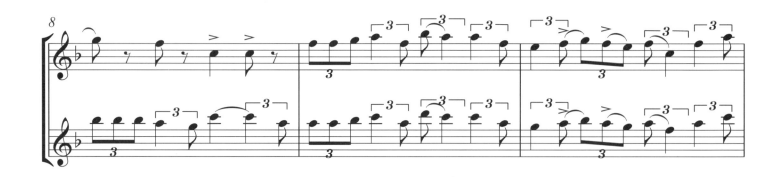

LOCH LOMOND

Traditional
arr. Florian Bramböck

Play-Along Flute – World Music

Cuba
Richard Graf & Richard Filz
Bolero, Son Montuno, Cha Cha, Mambo, Rumba

UE 31551

Ireland
arr. Richard Graf
The Foggy Dew, The Wind that Shakes the Barley,
The Wild Rover, Danny Boy, TheConnaughtman's Rambles

UE 31554

Israel
arr. Timna Brauer & Elias Meiri
Hava Nagila, Dror yikra, Ahavat Hadassa,
Tchiribim Tchiribom, Shalosh bnot hapele

UE 31572

Russia
arr. Ivan Malachovsky
Kalinka, Black Eyes, The Moon is Shining, Steppe all Around, Valenky

UE 31574

Scotland
arr. James Rae
Scotland the Brave, My Love is Like a Red, Red Rose,
The Skye Boat Song, Mhairi's Wedding, 100 Pipers

UE 31560

Brazil
Jovino Santos Neto
Choro da Luz, Quebrasamba, Maracatu, Cantigas de Roda, Coco

UE 31573

Argentina
Diego Collatti
Tango, Vals Criollo, Milonga, Zamba, Chacarera

UE 31567

Madagascar
HAJAmadagascar & August Schmidhofer
Apondo, E! Ralinina, O! Dralako, Zahoravo, Fiainana

UE 31564

Klezmer
arr. Yale Strom
The Silver Crown, Ma Yofes, Stoliner Nign, Romanian Hora, Dorohoi Khusidl

UE 31570

Christmas
Richard Graf
We Wish You a Merry Christmas, O Sanctissima (O du Fröhliche),
Zumba, zum, Il est né, le divin Enfant, O Tannenbaum,
Jingle Bells, Vamos pastorcillos, Stille Nacht, Aguinaldo Ricardo

UE 32693

www.**u**niversal**e**dition.com
vienna · london · new york

730/V 06

MAGIC FLUTE
on stage

Notenbüchlein der ANNA MAGDALENA BACH

eingerichtet für Flöte und Klavier von / arranged for flute and piano by
Ulrich Müller-Doppler & Peter Ludwig

- Schwierigkeitsgrad Anfänger bis Mittel
- eine ideale Einführung in barocke Spielweisen und Interpretationen

- for beginners to middle grade players
- an ideal introduction to Baroque techniques and interpretation

UE 32 921

Erik Satie
3 GYMNOPÉDIES

für Flöte und Klavier / for flute and piano
eingerichtet von / transcribed by
Sylvia C. Rosin

UE 32 988

Peter Iljitsch Tschaikowsky
KINDERALBUM

eingerichtet für Flöte und Klavier von / arranged for flute and piano by
Ulrich Müller-Doppler & Peter Ludwig

UE 33 092

www.universaledition.com
vienna · london · new york

Universal Querflöten Edition

UE-Nr.

Flöte solo

18023	**J.S. Bach**	Partita a-Moll BWV1013, Sonate C-Dur BWV1033, für Flöte solo (Braun) [3/4]
18027	**C.Ph.E. Bach**	Sonate a-Moll Wq.132 für Flöte solo (Nastasi) [3/4]
17289	**G. Braun**	Magnificat für Flöte (od. Altflöte in G) [3]
17259	**C. Halffter**	„Debla" für Flöte solo [5]
17285	**W. Heider**	Drei Flöten-Ornamente [5]
17298	**A. Hugot**	25 Grandes Etudes op. 13 für Flöte (Vester), Bd. I (Etüden 1–12) [4]
18022		– Bd. II (Etüden 13–25) [4]
15970	**E. Karkoschka**	„Im Dreieck" f. 3 Flöten oder einen Flötisten u. Stereo-Tonträger [4/5]
16943	**K. Lechner**	Septuplum für Flöte solo (Altflöte in G) [3/4]
13424	**J.W. Morthenson**	„Down" für Soloflöte [5]
18035	**H. Zender**	Angezogen vom Ton der Flöte. Drei Stücke für Flöte nach japanischen Zen-Sprüchen [5]

2 Flöten

18030	**J.S. Bach**	15 zweistimmige Inventionen, für 2 Flöten (Kolman) [3]
17288	**B. Bartók**	18 Flötenduos (Csupor) [1/2]
19491	**A.B.T. Berbiguier**	21 leichte Duette (Gerlof) [1/3]
18024	**Birtwistle, H.**	Duets for Storab [4]
18664	**M. Blavet**	Duette nach Werken von G.F. Händel (Betz) [2/3]
18675		Duette nach Werken von J.-Ph. Rameau (Betz) [1/2]
19492		Leichte Duette (Betz) [1/2]
19500	**A. Corelli**	Fünf Duette nach op. 5 Nr. 7–11 f. 2 Flöten nach einer Ausgabe v. 1740 (Braun) [2]
19485	**E.-F. Gebauer**	Drei Duos op. 24 (Gerlof) [2]
18036	**J. Haydn**	„Die Jahreszeiten" f. 2 Flöten (nach einer zeitgenöss. Bearbeitung) [3]
18037–18038		6 Duette (Faksimileausgabe), 2 Bände [3/4]
17282	„	Die Schöpfung" für 2 Flöten oder Violinen nach einer Ausgabe von 1806 (Füssl) [3]
18029	**H. Jelinek**	Vier Kanons für 2 Flöten aus dem Zwölftonwerk op. 15/6 (Braun) [4]
16737	**W.A. Mozart**	„Die Entführung aus dem Serail" f. 2 Flöten nach einer Ausg. von 1799 (Braun) [3]
16773		„Die Hochzeit des Figaro" für 2 Flöten nach einer Ausgabe von 1799 (Braun) [3]
15966		„Die Zauberflöte" für 2 Flöten nach einer Ausgabe von 1792 (Braun) [3]
17284		„Don Giovanni" für 2 Flöten nach einer Ausgabe um 1809 (Braun) [3]
17297		Variationen über „Ah! vous dirai-je, Maman" KV 300e (265) für 2 Flöten (Kolman) [2/3]
16742	**G. Rossini**	„Der Barbier von Sevilla" für 2 Flöten nach einer Ausgabe von 1820 (Füssl) [3]
16734	**J.L. Tulou**	Drei Duos op.14 für 2 Flöten (Braun) [2]
19488	**J.B. Vanhal**	„Die Bedrohung und Befreiung der k.k. Haupt- und Residenzstadt Wien", Ausgabe für 2 Flöten (Hünteler) [2]
16997		Sechs Duette (Bryan), Bd. I (Nr. 1–3) [1/2]
16998		– Bd. II (Nr. 4–6) [1/2]
18672	**C.M. von Weber**	„Der Freischütz", Ausgabe für 2 Flöten von Diabelli 1822 (Hünteler) [3/4]
18040	**Wranitzky, P.**	6 Duos op. 11 (Faksimile-Ausgabe) [2/3]

3 und mehr Flöten

16995	**L. Gianella**	Quartett in G-Dur op. 52 für 4 Flöten (Imbescheid) [2/3]
16999		Zwei Trios op. 27 für 3 Flöten (Imbescheid) [3]
15970	**E. Karkoschka**	„Im Dreieck" f. 3 Flöten oder einen Flötisten u. Stereo-Tonträger [4/5]
17293	**R. Kelterborn**	Terzett für Querflöten [3/4]

Flöte und Klavier (Cembalo)

18025	**J.S. Bach**	Partita c-Moll BWV997, für Flöte und Cembalo (Petrenz) [3/4]
17294		Zwei Sonaten BWV1034, 1035 für Flöte und B.c. (Braun/Petrenz) [3/4]
17295		Zwei Sonaten BWV1030, 1032 f. Flöte u. Cembalo(Braun/Petrenz)[3/4]
18662	**J.S. Bach/C.Ph.E. Bach**	Sonate Es-Dur BWV1031, Sonate g-Moll BWV1020 für Flöte und obligates Cembalo (Braun/Petrenz) [3]
18666	**Bartók/Arma**	Suite paysanne Hongroise für Flöte und Klavier [3/4]
18031	**N. Beecroft**	Tre pezzi brevi für Flöte und Klavier (Harfe/Gitarre) [4/5]
18028	**L. v. Beethoven**	Drei Sonaten op.12 f. Flöte u. Klavier ges. v. Drouet (Braun)[3/4]
15967		Sonate F-Dur op.17 für Flöte und Klavier (Braun) [2/3]
31851–31853		Drei Sonaten op.30, Band 1–3, für Flöte und Klavier einger. v. Drouet (Braun) [4]
17290		Serenade op.8, arr. von Th. Böhm f. Flöte u. Klavier (Imbescheid) [3/4]
17287	**M. Blavet**	Sonate e-Moll op. 3/III für Flöte und B.c. (Klavier) (Bauer/Bach) [3]
15971	**Th. Böhm**	Fantasie op. 21 über ein Thema von Schubert für Flöte und Klavier (Braun) [4/5]
17292	**H. Bornefeld**	„Im Dutzend billiger", 12 harmlose Stücke f. Flöte u. Klavier(Braun)[1/2]
18668	**L. de Caix d'Hervelois**	Suite A-Dur op. 6 Nr. 1 f. Flöte u. B.c. (Waechter/Petrenz) [3]
19498	**N. Chédeville**	Zwei Suiten für Flöte und B.c. (König/Petrenz) [2/3]
19496	**A. Corelli**	La Follia (op. 5/XII) für Flöte und B.c. (Heidecker/Petrenz) [3]
30273–30275		Sechs Sonaten op. 5 für Flöte und B.c. nach einer Ausgabe von 1740, Bd. I–III (Braun/Petrenz) [3]
16954	**C. Debussy**	„Bilitis", für Flöte und Klavier (Lenski) [3]
17299		Prélude à l'après-midi d'un faune, für Flöte und Klavier (Lenski) [3/4]